WOMEN IN BUSINESS

WOMEN IN BUSINESS

7 Successful Communication Tips To Enhance Your Career

(+ Specific Observations From our Male Counterparts . . .)

PJ Pierce, Ph.D.

To order additional copies of this book, contact:
Xlibris Corporation
1-888-795-4274
www.Xlibris.com
Orders@Xlibris.com
58422

Contents

To all the outstanding, professional women I have worked with who continue to search for that delicate balance of successful communication skills at work and home, *and* to all the outstanding, professional men who have contributed their constructive and honest feedback to this book.

Women in Business: *Ten Communication Tips To Enhance Your Career* is lovingly dedicated to Matt, Pete, Jane, and a special spiritual shout-out to Dr. Joseph (Buzzy)Pierce.

Introduction

In Ram Charan's and Geoffrey Colvin's article in *Fortune Magazine*, "Why CEO's Fail," the authors found *that unsuccessful executives put strategy before people.* Successful executives did not shine in the areas of planning or finances—*they were successful because they demonstrated integrity, assertiveness, effective communication and trust-building behaviors.*

If women want to be frequent players at the senior management level, the competencies mentioned by Charan and Colvin are all about communication skills: integrity reveals itself in the use of power. Assertive behavior is one of the most important communication behaviors, and trust building behaviors reflect themselves in the use of interpersonal communication such as listening with empathy and learning to resolve conflicts.

I have personally observed many female executives who, once given the title and power that accompanies it, make the worst mistakes with power, resulting in chaos and under-realized results. And, of course, I have seen other female executives accept the mantle and press on with demonstrated integrity, assertive behaviors that did not hurt the people or the situation, provide excellent communication and trust-building behaviors, and have team collaboration beyond their most optimistic dreams.

Tell your team what your communication style is and how you'd like to communicate in the workplace—let them know the best way to communicate with you. One manager I worked for many years ago, said, "I'm not going to answer my phone messages, so you'll have to ask for time in my office face-to-face or put it in an email." That seems unrealistic in this world of texting, Blackberry's, etc. However, the major point is tell your team the best way to get to you and make decisions with you. It's so essential to excellent communication. That is my purpose: to provide you the benefit of my observations of successful female executives who have had well-oiled teams working for them on a long-term basis. The 7 Key Communication Skills that I believe can enhance your career all come from those observations and interviews with many professionals over a 35 year span.

Emphasis on the Work—women are sometimes so mired down in the Work that they forget that it's a game of strategy that men know and love instinctively. GI Joe was not about plastic warriors—it was about developing the strategy that led to the enemy's demise. (I watched my sons in action quite a few times.) Women, on the other hand, burrow down and get a pile of Work done, as the man works the system and climbs ahead much faster using his strategic skills to get there. Charan and Colvin are saying that the first persons to combine both skill sets of strategy AND communication skills will be the victor, and I agree completely. Let's see how this success strategy can take place.

> *"Inside of you is a smart, powerful, dynamic, capable, self-confident, alive, alert, fabulous woman. Let her come out and play. The world is waiting for you."*
>
> *—Louis Hay, Empowering Women, Hay House, 1997.*

It's All About Perception

> *"To improve your own perception, actively question the accuracy of your own perceptions, seek more information to verify, talk with people before forming the perception, and realize that perception changes over time."*
>
> Kathleen S. Verderber and Rudolph F, Verderber, Inter-Act, Wadsworth Publishing, 2001.

Perception Checking:

Perception checking in an important communication skill to use in the business world. According to Verderber and Verderber, " . . . our perceptions come from the selection, organization, and interpretation of sensory information. Inaccurate perceptions cause us to see the world not as it is—but as we would like it to be." I know I have been incorrect in many situations when I made a snap judgment about someone and his or her ability to help the team. It's only when you continue to have patience, check your initial perceptions with good questioning and listening skills, and constantly wait for the complete person to emerge (especially during the crisis times) that you know you have been correct in your overall assessment.

Negative perceptions can happen when the following three behaviors surface. Coaching of the individual could greatly assist in her overall business professional perception.

1. Giggling at the end of a sentence
2. Making things "little"
3. Hedging

Perception of giggling: out of control, out of touch,
not intellectual, unprofessional

Giggling during the communication becomes a habit like "um" or "like". Women who are guilty of this don't even hear it anymore, and coaching can be very effective by taping the person and letting her hear how unprofessional this sounds.

Perception of making things "little": unsure, unimportant

Women have a tendency to ask for a "little" favor . . . . "let's all wear our "little black dresses" tonight . . . . heard on the TV the other day a woman ask for a "little donation", hoping, I guess, that it wouldn't take too much away from our little pocketbooks. Please observe and hear this—it definitely diminishes your professional demeanor.

Perception of hedging: indecisive, not in control, don't care,
unable to commit

Hedging is giving the perception of being indecisive and not able to say yes or no without any type of extra qualifiers. Commit! Don't worry about being Miss Perfect—get out there and be decisive— you will be applauded for this by men and women. I think it stems from women not being able to be wrong, so they hedge.

Hedging: "Where would you like to eat tonight?" "Oh . . . . anywhere . . . . I don't care . . . . wherever you want to go . . . ." (then he or she makes a decision; the hedger complains about the decision, which creates the deadly "script" that continues into an argument.).

Decisive: "Do you want to go to Paragon tonight" "Yes, I'd love to." "No, thank you; I have other plans."

Hedging: "How many books are on the table, Ann?" Oh. About 3.

Decisive: "How many books are on the table, Ann?" 4 books, John.

Outer Appearance:

It still counts in the overall perception of someone. So many TV shows have had immediate success with makeovers, etc. Regardless of how you feel about these shows, I always try to remember that it's about self esteem. If it makes you push those shoulders back and walk a little taller, then why not? In business, carriage and a sense of confidence does make an impression. I can still remember the way a person walked down the hall with the confidence of a CEO—he *did* become our CEO, and has moved on to other successful positions as well.

Shaking Hands:

Know how to shake hands properly—many of you wonder why I am putting in such a basic skill, but my informal research bears this out. Every time I teach a class, I stand by the door and shake hands, on purpose, to assess this most important skill. Sometimes women will put their hands out flat to me; I had a male colleague tell me once that he didn't know whether to kiss it or turn it around and shake it!

Place your fingers forward as an extension of your arm with your thumb on top. Place your hand all the way back into the outstretched hand of the other—all the way, so that your thumb touches their thumb. Give a firm grip, but not too strong. You need to practice this if you're not comfortable. True, some men try to give too firm a grip, or they are afraid of "hurting" you and give a limp grip instead. You extend your hand in every situation—there are many men over 50 who are unsure of what to do—you are the one who needs to shake hands in a social or business situation and make the other person feel comfortable. You need to take the lead in this area—enough said!

Add your vocal tones to the "package", and we're definitely getting somewhere. Your vocal variety, vocal tones, and your ability to sound powerful are all skills that you can achieve with friends who will be honest with their feedback and a tape recorder.

Thinking Styles

Wonder why you always clashed with a particular teacher or friend? Your thinking pattern was most likely the complete opposite of the other person's way of approaching a project. *An effective communicator/leader needs to understand his or her thinking style and have respect for others who may not think the same way.* The "check & balance" is necessary for any successful operation.

Example:

Putting together an outdoor grill for the patio can be a challenge if the thinking styles are opposed to each other. One, for instance, likes to read the manual and go step by step through the process. If there is a washer or screw left, he or she will stay next to the grill and find the piece that is missing until midnight comes and you have to infuse food periodically. Their partner, by the way, doesn't care if there is a washer or screw extra and is enjoying pizza and TV inside the house—just so it works they say.

The person who needs every detail in this puzzle solved is an inductive thinker, one who needs all the details building up to the Big Picture. The person eating pizza is the deductive, or Big Picture person—he or she too can go into the details, but the Big Picture usually suffices to get the job done. Thus the clash between thinkers on this small project or even a larger one—knowing which type of thinker you are provides insight into communication with another. The point is that there are many ways to get a project completed, and both types of thinker can make this project successful. You need both Big Picture (Deductive) and Detailed (Inductive) Thinkers.

Inductive Thinking

- Builds with details to Big Picture
- Enjoys structure and adding detail

- Frustrated/confused unless this thought process is followed
- Shrubs, flowers, then Forest

Deductive Thinking

- Big Picture first
- Frustrated with the detailed approach
- Builds from Big Picture when details are needed
- Forest, then shrubs and flowers

Introduction Summary
It's All About Perception

- Be patient in your perception checking
- No giggling or making things "little" and especially no hedging
- Preparation of your outer appearance is important
- Know how to shake hands properly
- Understand how important your handshake is to your overall perception
- Be aware of Inductive and Deductive Thinking Styles and how they affect the outcome of good communication with others

Practice How to be "Heard"

> "Managing your communication skills and being aware of their importance is so essential—it doesn't matter whether we are reading, writing, speaking, or listening—great leaders step up and converse *with* their audiences and create a relationship, recognizing the need for clear, honest, and effective communication."
>
> PJ Pierce, *Successful Management Communications*, University of Dayton's Center for Leadership & Executive Development, 2009.

Speaking—Power Tone:

Learn to introduce yourself with the *power tone*. First, *clear your throats*. The tone you hear is the sound you need to use for credibility's sake . . . not to sound like "little men", but your tone in a meeting, a presentation, etc. needs to have a pleasantly-low tone for the perception of being under control. I am involved in an interesting set of meetings right now where the emotion is high—one of the Board members mentioned to me that I sounded clear and level-headed when inside I was screaming at the antagonist, "What are you thinking?" It's all a matter of perception . . . that includes your outer wear, your body language and your tone, most of all.

Second, let's take tone to another level and add a simple but crucial part of the perception. *Learn to say your own name as you are being introduced.* Many women try to sound like this . . . . Hi (tone high and ingratiating), I'm Tammy Shaw, (voice very high/ questioning tone on Shaw) AND I'm from ABC Company (again, another high or questioning tone on Company)!

Do this: Good morning (pleasantly low on morning), I'm Tammy Shaw (pleasantly low on Shaw) from ABC Company (pleasantly low on Company). This downward tone or power tone used at the end of your name can then be expanded into making important points, etc. You WILL be heard in the group—just don't overdo it! This translates to home as well. "Just wait until your father gets home . . . . or Matt, come here please, now (pleasantly low power tone). I tried it on my own sons (when they were much younger), and it works. They tune you out if you give it too much verbiage and too much high-sounding tones. Listen carefully to your local newscasters regarding this *power tone*. They all have it, and they are masters of bridging to the next topic as well. We'll address that skill in the presenting tip.

Two other areas of interest when speaking are:

1. *Stop talking in run-on sentences*
2. *Learning to respectfully interrupt*

According to my observations, women *have a tendency to talk in run-on sentences*, using AND for several minutes. Perhaps it is cultural, where they "can't get a word in", so they rattle on forever when they get the floor. However, this is something you need to change—if you want to talk this way with your friends on the phone, no problem. But you will have to switch when you come into your business environment. There's nothing so irritating as to have to listen to a long-winded explanation, when the response could have been handled in a brief sentence.

Learning to interrupt is difficult for women, who have been taught since they were very young not to do this! At our dinner table in the 60's, my father would say, "Five minutes for you, Patty, five minutes for you Jane, five minutes for you Fred, and five minutes for you, Joe." We were allowed to talk and tell about our day, but there was a limit to this speaking. I guess I learned to say what I had to say in that limit; my father, an engineer, was setting parameters on us—it taught us to net it out, to express ourselves carefully, not to interrupt, and to understand others needed a turn as well.

Thus, the reason I am suggesting that you may have to interrupt because not all of us grew up that way—men have a tendency to talk over us. When *Men in Business* is published, there will an entire section on their inability to listen and wait to speak. The important thing to do is when that happens, interrupt and say, "John, you interrupted Sally—I'd like to hear what she had to say." We need to interrupt respectfully and support other women (and men) when the stronger communicator takes over.

Put your hand up and say "STOP—I need to hear what Carolyn had to say."

Writing:

Learning to "be heard" in your emails is to get to the point—be DEDUCTIVE in your approach with every email message—"My purpose in writing is . . . ." Give them the Big Picture first. No one has the time to search it out.

In this day of texting directly from phones without spelling, etc., it is difficult to return to email and send a coherent message. However, it will be very important, especially if you are communicating with senior management, an international client, etc. The following are some tips that could help you be heard:

- Use the person's name within the first 15 words of your message, and end with the international phrase "Best regards" or "Regards".
- Spell-check should be used. Don't send it out before you re-read or spell-check your message.
- Include the original message in your response, so that the context is there in front of the person.
- Take your time. Because e-mail is so "fast", don't fall into that trap. You never know how many times someone will send your original message to another within the organization.
- Write the way you would as if the person were sitting in your office face to face. No CAPS, please. You're shouting at me.
- Use common sense when greeting with a first and/or last name. Stay on the conservative side if the message is to an

international audience. Formality and proper word choice is more important outside the U.S.—sense of humor is different as well.

- If the e-mail is being sent to another country, please be very aware of idioms and slang—it may offend the other person, because they'll have "no clue" what the message is.
- Use the Subject line for the urgency of the communication.
- *Faux pas*: Not labeling the subject line, not responding promptly, not coming to the point quickly with the purpose, being verbose, placing urgent when it was not, not listing your phone or fax #'s, using humor which could be misconstrued as sarcasm, not being selective about your audience.

Resource: Ann Marie Sabath, *Email Etiquette Tips, Business Etiquette in Brief*, 1998.

Observe how the inductively-prepared email is revised to be "heard". The subject line reveals the overall purpose, which is not revealed until the 3rd paragraph.

Inductive Email:

Subject: Kudos

In the past 4 months we have been working hard to manage the execution of the Resources Exit Plan (REP) using the Leopard technology platform.

Deployment will be in place starting December 8. The rollout includes several LEO units that will need collaboration and support from the SAB worldwide.

I'd like to take this opportunity to thank John Riverson on the ground and his team for developing the REP plan and his patience under fire during 2008.

Cheers,
Ann Smith

Revised Deductive Email:

Subject: Kudos to John Riverson & Team

My purpose is to thank John Riverson and his team for the deployment of the REP Program Plan during the last quarter of 2008. We appreciate his patience and perseverance.

Job well done!

Best regards,
Ann Smith

Rollout: December 8, 2008   Worldwide, 100 countries

Communication Tip #1 Summary: Practice How To Be "Heard"

- Speaking: use the Power Tone at work and home
- Speaking: try to work on your run-on sentences
- Speaking: when all else fails, learn how to respectfully interrupt
- Writing: get to the point in all your messages, especially email—be direct and succinct
- Writing: don't press the "send" button on an emotional message until you breathe & count to 10, or set aside until an hour later & re-read
- Writing: All Email is public. All Cell phones could be public. All Photos are public.
- Writing: think benefits when you write. Many times you are in the selling mode, trying to persuade a group of people to do something for you—they need assurance and the benefits to them

Use STARR Power To Present

"What the Greek leader Pericles said nearly 2,500 years ago is just as true today: 'One who forms a judgment on any point but cannot explain it clearly might as well never have thought of at all on
the subject.'"

Stephen E. Lucas. *The Art of Public Speaking*, p.2—quoted from Richard Whatley, *Elements of Rhetoric*, 7th edition (London: John W. Parker, 1846), p.10.

So much has been written on presentation skills; many times it's not the formal presentation that sells the message—it's the extemporaneous meeting where it counts. As your boss stops you in the hall and asks about a specific project or program you are working on, you will sound so credible and "put together".

The STARR approach is from the American Management Association's materials. It is a master template that helps you get your thoughts in line so that you can respond extemporaneously to management in the hallway, the proverbial elevator, or in a well-crafted presentation.

S   stands for here's the SITUATION
T   stands for here are the TASKS that I am working on
A   stands for here are the ACTIONS my team has taken
R   stands for here are the RESULTS as of right now

And you may be asked on the spot for recommendations,

R   stands for the RECOMMENDATIONS we have at this time.

You will be perceived as a good communicator, organized, and knowledgeable, all at the same time! The following information includes the results of an informal survey I conducted to determine presentation structures for presenters. There is a great deal of frustration that takes place when a manager walks into your cubicle and asks for a presentation to be developed and gives no guidance for developing it—kind of a "shot in the dark," which wastes time and energy of all involved. This approach frustrated many of my presenting class, so I surveyed over 100 executives to find out how they wanted information presented. The following are the results of that survey, illustrating a technical, sales, and senior management outline. For a general audience, the structure can be a combination of any of the above, based on some informal needs assessments before the presentation is given.

Outlines for Different Audiences

Technical Audience

Roadmap:

(Topic, what I want you to *do* with this information, timeframe and Q&A format (ask questions anytime or have time at the end for Q's)

Body:

- ❑ Background
- ❑ Statement of the Problem/Situation
- ❑ Procedure
- ❑ Analysis
- ❑ Solutions
- ❑ Conclusions
- ❑ Recommendations

Summary/Conclusion

Sales-Oriented Audience

Roadmap:

(Topic, what I want you to *do* with this information, timeframe and Q&A format: ask questions anytime or have time at the end for Q's)

Body:

- ❏ Identify and clarify the business need
- ❏ Customer Testimonial
- ❏ Features and Functions
- ❏ Benefits
- ❏ Proof
- ❏ Ask for the Order—Closing

Summary/Conclusion

Senior-Level Management

Roadmap:

(Topic, what I want you to *do* with this information, timeframe and Q&A format: ask questions anytime or have time at the end for Q's)

Body:

- ❑ Purpose and action needed
- ❑ Brief description of the plan
- ❑ Business Impact
- ❑ Return on Investment
- ❑ Risk Analysis
- ❑ Recommendations
- ❑ Validation and Feedback for Next Steps

Summary/Conclusion

Now you're ready for the Q&A session:

This is the trickiest and most important part of your presentation plan. Be on your toes! *Actually click into another gear for the Q&A, and listen intently.*

1. Stand up. Don't sit down. You'll get caught being too relaxed—have a notepad ready for the 2-part questions you will receive.
2. Learn to manage the Q&A session—there are many who could dominate this session and leave out the rest of the audience—you are the facilitator.
3. Be ready with at least 10 anticipated questions.
4. Clarify the intent of the question, and answer it based on time limitations.
5. Ask whether you were able to answer it to the person's satisfaction. If not, don't show offense—coolly take if off-line for additional detail.
6. Learn to say "I don't know"—we can't be expected to know everything. However, the point is to give the person a timeframe for answering it. "I'm unsure of the complete answer to that, Jack, but I'll get back to you with more detail on Friday by 3:00."

Alan Perlman has a wonderful book out with *Perfect Phrases for Executive Presentations*. New York: McGraw-Hill, 2006. He has provided various phrases for *After the Q&A:*

- "Thank you again for inviting me. I hope that what I've said has prompted some questions—let's get to them.
- Thank you very much for this opportunity to speak with you. I would now be pleased to head any questions you may have.
- Thank you again for inviting me today. Now let's get to the comments and questions.
- Thanks for your attention—now let's open it up for your questions and comments."

PJ's Top Ten Presenting Reminders:

1. Mix with the audience before you present so they get to know you—you are there for your audience, not vice versa.
2. Do your homework on your audience's needs and backgrounds—anticipate at least 10 questions people may ask you, and design the structure of your presentation for your audience.
3. Never make excuses or apologies.
4. Involve the audience with a question or activity.
5. Use body language, movement, and vocal variety.
6. Never read slides word for word—paraphrase.
7. Use transitions between thoughts/slides—an advanced skill that separates you from the other presenters.
8. Take breaks after each 45 minute segment and end on time.
9. Be flexible, pay attention to the room setup and technical needs.
10. Always have a Roadmap and what you want the audience to DO with your presentation material (To entertain? To provide benefits? To persuade for a new program? To provide important technical results?) Always be prepared for the Q&A.

The last reminder on PJ's Top Ten List regarding the preparation for the Q&A is dear to my heart, since the learning from this episode impacted my entire career. My manager at NCR was Bill Julian, the consummate professional. We were due to meet with the VP of Education/Training regarding the development of an important course entitled "Effective Presentation Techniques" that would be taught to the worldwide sales force. Bill knew that it was an important meeting, and he asked me to prepare 10 questions that the VP could ask about the project. Then we rehearsed them, and I was feeling pretty relaxed. Then he asked for 10 additional questions with rehearsal, which surprised me, but I complied. The good news is that the project was approved!

How many of the 20 questions do you believe the VP asked? Many say 4; others say 12, but the true answer is that 17 of the 20 were asked & answered to his satisfaction, and I was truly thankful for Bill's guidance. I hold myself to that standard today as I prepare for a major presentation, project review, or training session!

Communication Tip #2 Summary:
Use STARR Power & Directness

❖ Senior management will come into the presentation asking what do you want me to **do** with this information? It is your job to present that answer upfront and then give details.

❖ STARR is the most effective way to give a status report extemporaneously.

❖ Giving a Roadmap upfront satisfies every type of audience. It includes: greeting, overall purpose of what is to be done with the info, time spent on content and how long for the Q&A.

❖ Eye contact is key.

❖ Don't make excuses or apologies.

❖ Know how to handle the Q&A.

❖ Know the audience and adjust your outline accordingly.

❖ An outstanding presenter converses with the audience & provides smooth transitions.

Listening For Information, Clarification and Empathy

> "Listen and respond very carefully . . . . every conversation has to count . . . *the conversation is the relationship* . . . one conversation at a time, you are building, destroying, or flat-lining your relationships."
>
> Susan Scott, *Fierce Conversations*. New York, Berkley Books, 2004.

Use Emotional Intelligence While You Listen

Emotional Intelligence is a relatively new term to add an additional communication dimension to an IQ, or "academic smarts". With an Emotional Quotient (EQ) which is equal to "emotional smarts", women can learn to communicate on an interpersonal level with individuals in any given situation, remaining calm and in control in the listening process.

(Key addresses regarding Emotional Intelligence can be found in the work of Daniel Goleman and the Hay Group: *www. hayresourcesdirect.haygroup.com*)

To hone our listening skills, we need to know how to listen without filters. When messages coming from others challenge us and our way of thinking, we tend to reject them. We "filter" messages, paying attention to some and ignoring others. Excellent listeners learn to focus, ask clarifying questions, exhibit excellent turn-taking, and give feedback that is clear as to their understanding and expectations of the situation.

We also need to learn to understand the **"150 wpm Rule"**:

The 150 wpm Rule refers to focusing on the person who is speaking, usually at 150 word per minute (wpm). This is not easy to do, because our mind is usually racing along at 450 wpm or more! That extra amount is 1) forming a response before the speaker is finished, 2) thinking about other things it would rather be doing, or 3) daydreaming because the message may not be inspiring!

I can honestly say that I have made out my grocery list, staring at an uninspiring speaker as if I were hanging on every word—shame! ☺ Next, I would like to give you a few tips for listening for information, for clarification, and especially for empathy, at 150 wpm, in various listening situations.

Listening For Information

- Make an effort to regularly listen at approximately **150 wpm**
- Schedule **silent brainstorming sessions** that will force you to listen to others after the ideas are produced
- Listen for the 5W's and the H: Who, What, Where, Why, When & How
- Pick up nuances of gossip vs. fact
- Accept and give *respect to the speaker*

Listening For Clarification

- Learn to paraphrase more than you usually do: "In other words, John, what I heard you say is that you recommend our buying this package as soon as possible. Is that correct?"
- Reflect (mirroring their words for clarification) "Taking all in account, you 'believe we must act now'—am I understanding you Jennifer?"

Silent brainstorming:

Get a wider range of ideas on the table and *listen for information and clarification:*

- Have everyone take a pack of small cards/Post It's
- Give the assignment of what you want to brainstorm w/o discussion
- Each new idea goes on a separate card
- Give the appropriate timeframe, and let persons silently work separately
- Organize into small teams of 4 or 5—Let each team find a place in the room
- Have each team find all the similar ideas and create one idea for it
- Take all ideas and either lay on the table or tape on the wall
- Listening to each other describe the ideas is next—key time, because the speaker must describe factually
- Silently, the team votes on the ones they prefer, based on the # of team members and the # of ideas:
- **Round 1:** If there are 4 people on a team, and there 28 ideas, divide the # of people on the team by the # of ideas. Then everyone has the opportunity to have 7 votes. They are encouraged to move around the table or wall making a check on the ideas they prefer, listening and asking questions to clarify.
- **Round 2:** The group will now have to tally the checkmarks and come up with 7 major ideas left. Now, since 4 goes into 7 more than once, allow the next round to have 2 votes by checkmarks, moving closer and closer to having 1 best idea.
- This process is democratic; it allows for listening; it allows for clarification; it allows for personalities to be taken out of the process, except in the clarification stage when the idea-maker must explain; however, the explanation needs to be kept factual, etc.

I have had great success with this process—it involves a high level of listening and clarification, which is the keystone to listening at 150 wpm.

Listening For Empathy

This particular skill is learned and needs practice—if you are in a management role, there may be many opportunities at work or at home when you may need to adopt the role of Empathic Listener. Professional counselors, police officers, social workers, and many other empathic listening-type professionals work tirelessly on this type of listening.

I was teaching an all-day seminar for young executives, and I heard from the back of the room, "I don't get it—my wife asks and asks for me to 'listen' to her this way—my answer is "if you want me to solve the problem for you, OK. If not, I just can't sit here and listen—football's on." So! Since I have heard this comment over and over for the past 35 years, I continue to give examples of empathic listening, because there must not be enough models in people's lives to teach this particular skill.

Empathic Listening is not asking for a resolution, a "fix" to a problem—it's more of a time for this person to reveal feelings that may be affecting your relationship.

- Listen and focus on the *person* and their feelings at 150 wpm—turn off your tendency to want to solve the problem, to "fix" it, or respond immediately, having constructed a response before they have finished their verbal thoughts to you—they don't want a response, just the knowledge that you really hear what they are saying.
- Listen *non-judgmentally*—by not immediately evaluating what was said, you can encourage a person to open up and give you new ideas
- Use *reflective listening* to help them to solve their own problems—examples include: "I see your point; I've been there myself"—many times the person gets clarity after they are "allowed" to speak without judgment
- Put your hand near your mouth (to signal self *not* to speak)
- Know that you are under no obligation to "solve" the problem

Thoughts About Empathy

When I ask you to listen to me and you start giving me advice, you have not done what I asked. You have immediately jumped to your management style of problem resolution or "fixing" the problem for me, and I don't need that right now.

When I ask you to listen to me, and you begin to tell me why I shouldn't feel that way, you are disrespecting my feelings.

When you accept that I feel what I feel, no matter how irrational, then I can quit trying to convince you and get about the business of understanding what's behind this irrational feeling. When that's clear, the answers are obvious, and I don't need advice.

Perhaps that's why prayer works for some people—because God is mute, and He/She doesn't give advice or try to fix things! "They" just listen and let you work it out for yourself.

Please listen—I just need your empathy.
—Cindy Joseph, University of Southern California, 2008.

Communication Tip #3 Summary:
Listen for Information, Clarification and Empathy

❖ Listening skills are more important as you reach senior level management than ever before.

❖ Pay attention to a balance of your EQ and your IQ when reaching this level.

❖ Silent brainstorming is an effective technique to assess creative thoughts.

❖ Stop your brain and listen at 150 wpm, or you will miss key thoughts being expressed.

❖ Understand that empathy is a vital part of the balanced executive.

Be Assertive, Not Aggressive

- You need to pull your own strings, or you are being manipulated by someone else.
- You are asking to be victimized when you place total reliance in someone else to control your life properly.
- Never expect to be understood by everyone—you will become a victim if you feel you need to prove yourself to other people.
- Live now. Accept not being understood by everyone all the time.
- *The more you avoid assertive behaviors, the more you teach others you are willing to be their victim.*
- Use the "I" statement for a positive, assertive result:

Wayne Dyer. *Pull Your Own Strings* (New York, Morrow & Co.), 2002.

According to Dyer, Victimizers are:

Drunks, bores, whiners, complainers, bullies, arguers, braggarts, admonishers, interrupters, shockers, fast talkers, reporters/squealers, insisters, guilt merchants, moody, greedy or jealous persons. He mentions several other key points:

- You get treated the way you teach people to treat you.
- Don't give up control of yourself to all those who would gladly take over the reins and you are willing to loosen the hold.
- This is my way. What's your way? THE way doesn't exist.
- You are a product of what you choose for yourself in any life situation.

- Pull your own strings and enjoy your life on Earth, OR let others pull the strings and spend life being upset and controlled by the victimizers of the world.

If women want to be tapped for leadership positions, the following are key characteristics needed for the job:

- In control of emotions
- Trusts the team members to get the job done
- Always finishes the assignment
- Communicates (on top of voice and e-mail—writes clear concise messages)
- Chooses good people
- Is a woman of her word (Integrity)
- Is the driving force
- Most prepared in the room
- Programmed to be successful

In addition to leadership characteristics, women need to adopt assertive behaviors (i.e. Standing up for yourself in a socially-accepted manner.)

- You have a right to get your core needs met in a relationship or at least not to have them violated.
- You have the right to ask dumb questions.
- You have the right not to be a victim.
- You have the right to confront issues that are troubling you.
- You have the right to disagree.
- You have the right to say yes.
- You have the right to say no.

Susan Scott, *Fierce Conversations.* New York, Berkley Books, 2004.

Example:

- Not good: Could I ask you a little question?
- Much better: *John, I have a question for you.*

Example:

- Really weak: Is it all right if I go out for an hour?
- Much better: *I'm going out for an hour, dear—bring you anything?*

Harriet Braiker said it best in *The Disease To Please* (New York: McGraw-Hill, 2001.)

- Don't say yes when you want to say no.
- I'll check on it . . . buy time.
- *Sandwich technique*—I'll check on it. I did. Thank you, no.
- Talk yourself out of Approval Addiction
- Learn to Delegate
- It's OK not to be nice
- Anger . . . . ask for time out to get under control.

Assertiveness is:

- Standing up for my rights and describing how I feel protects me from resentment, stress and anger.
- Considering the other person allows me to avoid unnecessary conflict and damage to the relationship.
- Application of the following Communications Skills: Listening, Clarification, Resolution, Consensus, Open Discussion, Being Direct, and *Using "I statements"* and "*In my opinion"* to assist in clear communication.

Assertiveness?

- If I don't understand a statement, I ask for clarification.   Yes
- I am more concerned with clarifying an idea then I am what anyone at the table thinks of me.   No
- I withhold remarks to my superior because I feel intimidated.   No
- When I disagree with others, I become angry and attack them.   No

- I only speak up when asked a direct question.   No
- If I don't agree with others, I withdraw from
  the conversation.   No
- I agree in the group, but outside the group,
  I undermine the agreements made.   No
- I only express my true feelings outside of work.   No
- I keep track of every negative comment,
  behavior, and action made by another person
  w/the purpose of sabotage when I have
  an opportunity.   No
- I praise & acknowledge others for their good
  ideas.   Yes
- I like to make black-and-white statements and
  tolerate no "gray", thinking that this behavior
  communicates to others that I'm being decisive.   No

Aggressive

- "Gunnysacking" (holding on to any perceived hurt w/future ideas of revenge)
- Verbal/Emotional aggression
- Physical aggression

Passive

- "Stuffing" all the perceived "hurts" inside
- Perception is all about ME
- Withdraw from the conflict situation—no resolution

Passive-Aggressive

- They are passive in the conference room, and the minute they get out in the hallway they are totally negative toward the person or the decision
- "I'm gonna get you, and you'll never see it coming."
- They find another way to hurt you.
- They never forget a perceived slight.

Scenarios:

#1

You are in a meeting, and the vice president presents a solution to a problem you had noticed also. You believe that you have a better idea to throw out for discussion.

- ❑ *Passive Response: (do nothing in the meeting and wish you had spoken up)*
- ❑ *Aggressive Response: (tell the boss that "I have a much better idea than that.")*
- ❑ *Passive-Aggressive: (say nothing, and then after the meeting in the hallway, mention to your colleagues that the VP's idea was stupid, and you had something much better to present.)*
- ❑ *Assertive Response: (ask in the meeting if the VP is accepting other options; if so, present in a respectful manner, not putting the VP's idea down.)*

#2

Your boss has invited you out to drinks with the "senior exec's" the same night that your son or daughter has the "big game."

- ❑ *Passive Response: (do nothing, don't RSVP, and don't go)*
- ❑ *Aggressive Response: ("Who does he think he is? I have a mind to go and dump a drink on his head for taking time away from my family.")*
- ❑ *Passive Aggressive: (says nothing, goes to the party, and then trashes the boss to the spouse on the way home.)*
- ❑ *Assertive Response: (#1: thanks the boss, goes to the party for 20 minutes and then heads to the Big Game. #2: thanks boss, but mentions the importance of his family plans already planned for several weeks and goes to the Big Game.)*

Communication Tip #4 Summary: Be Assertive, Not Aggressive

❖ Assertiveness is standing up for yourself in a socially-accepted manner; it is not aggressive behavior, which intends to "hurt" someone, either emotionally, physically, or psychologically.

❖ Gunnysacking is one of the most aggressive and hurtful behaviors to continue—for you and for others.

❖ Passive-aggressive behavior is selfish, "gaming" at its best, and never leads to authentic communication.

Understand Competition & Practice Collaboration

> "Would like to see non-competitive women acknowledge competition as a motivator in certain areas—they were taught that it was un-ladylike."
>
> Professional Women's Communication Skills Survey answer, 2009.

Even though you may not be a competitive person, you must learn the "rules of play"—if you have been on athletic teams as you were growing up, or if you played several sports in college, you are in a space to understand the competitive nature of business and your colleagues. I was lucky enough to have a father who taught the competitive and finesse aspects of tennis to my brothers and me. We understood what it was like to play in tournaments, what it was like to win and/or lose with grace, and how it felt to have others' eyes on you to produce a result. He was such a good influence at the time when fathers were mentoring their sons but not always the daughters. I understand competition, but I also learned the gentle practice of collaboration from my mother who was your typical PTA president, scout leader, and cookie chair.

These concepts are indeed paradoxes, but you need both to be successful in business and in life. Take competition—the United Way campaign started, and as usual, the divisions of my corporation made it into a NASCAR race, with the pictorial "head" on each racecar being a Sr. VP. Of course—what else but competition between divisions? I remember distinctly a woman on the committee say, "This is so silly . . . . always a competition . . . . can't we stop this somehow?!"

Understand the "rules of play", which include competition, direct talk, succinctness, no drama, and money is good. Women are no longer expected to stay in administrative roles where support is the main role. After you leave the cocoon of support, get ready to strategize, play politics, and contemplate how to produce a product that makes money.

In order to survive in this new world, sharpen up your teaming and communication skills.

Work Team Roles:

First, understand what a team process can be:

- Forming, Storming, Norming, Performing

Every successful team leader I know has had successful teams work through these phases. Well-oiled teams have leaders who understand the competitive nature of people, understand that you have to have collaboration and healthy competition, and a leader with superb strategic planning and communication skills. Women are ready for these jobs! Women are excellent planners and communicators!

Watch the pitfalls of GroupThink:

- Teams rush to conclusions without discussing the alternatives.
- The decisions are not carefully examined, even though there are risks.
- The team spends little time discussing reasons the alternatives were rejected.
- Members create rationalizations to avoid dealing directly with warnings.
- The team puts pressure on anyone who expresses doubt or questions the team's proposal.
- Members censure their own doubts.
- Members believe everyone is in unanimous agreement without testing that premise.

Understand Group Task Roles:

- Initiating, Elaborating
- Coordinating, Summarizing
- Recording, Evaluation
- Giving or Seeking Information
- Opinion Giving
- Clarifying, Consensus Taking
- Proposing Procedure

Recognize Group Maintenance Roles:

- Encouraging, Supporting
- Harmonizing, Gate-keeping (protecting information/persons)
- Process Observing, Setting Standards
- Tension Relieving

Deal with Selfish Behaviors:

- Blocking, Aggressiveness, Withdrawing, Dominating, Recognition Seeking
- Special Interest Pleading

Harris, Thomas and Sherblom, John C. *Small Group and Team Communication.* (Allyn and Bacon, Boston, Massachusetts: 2002, pp. 49-50.)

Women can understand competition and manage conflict:

Western societies expect conflict as part of the communication process because of our **competitive** nature/culture.

> Ex. "I will win this argument, at all costs." "I am unable to say I'm sorry, because that will show weakness."

Verderber, Kathleen and Verderber, Rudolph, Inter-Act, Wadsworth, 2001.

Women can collaborate:

Collaboration is the key to resolving conflicts, and many times it can be paradoxical in a conflict situation with competitiveness. Conflict should be expected—however, the important key is to teach your team members how to resolve it.

Dealing With Conflict

When dealing with difficult cases, the overall word to remember is *respect and honest, on-going communication.* You must not back away from constructive feedback—it is essential for the growth of the person and the team. If a person has accepted the constructive feedback and makes an attempt to correct the situation, he or she feels valued and respected—thus, many difficult situations can be averted.

However, if the person continues to be difficult, then his or her agenda could be to "win" at all costs. The goal needs to be one of not winning but establishing some compromise or collaborative action that creates as much of what each of you wants as possible. *If your goal is not win-win, you lose.*

Phil McGraw, Ph.D. *Self Matters*, 2002.

Types of Conflict:

- Pseudo—teasing that escalates
- Fact—factual information rules the day
- Value—different value conflicts are difficult, stemming from religion, politics, etc.
- Policy—this type of conflict can be maintained, once the policy is accepted
- Ego—difficult conflict but can be managed with coaching and counseling

Styles of Managing Conflict:

- Withdrawing   Avoiding, lose-lose
- Accommodating   Smoothing, lose-win

- Forcing   Competing, win-lose
- Compromising   Lose/lose or win-win
- Collaborating   Confronting, win-win

Verderber, Kathleen and Verderber, Rudolph, *Inter-Act*, Wadsworth Publishing, 2001.

Ways to Manage Conflict:

1. **Own the problem and have an open agenda regarding the situation**: "Help me understand it from your point of view." **Not** "We have a problem."
2. **Anticipate questions from your employees, and avoid evaluating the other person's motives.**
3. **Take deep breaths** (really count to 10 before you confront the other person—plan what you want to say)
4. **Watch your tone**. Use an empathic tone—speak slower than you normally would—do not use the "power" tone that you use during certain supervisory functions such as a presentation, etc.
5. **Paraphrase** it as long as you need to get to the problem (the "real" conflict in many cases may be hiding.)
6. Describe the behavior in terms of **behavior, consequence, and feelings.** "You went around me to make the critical decision to use John in the faculty presentation. As a consequence, half of the audience was confused with the change. By not telling me, I was feeling that you trying to undermine me."
7. Keep **discussion on issues**, not personal evaluation.
8. Both of you get **equal time** to tell your side of the perceived conflict.
9. Establish a **mediation action plan** if one is needed for the next step.

Example: Put the "Moose on the Table"

"Putting the moose on the table" is the act of addressing something that is "big, smelly, and no one wants to deal with"—the team leader and group have ignored it, because they have no idea how to resolve the conflict, either between two personalities, two groups, etc. By placing a small stuffed moose on the table, everyone laughs, and the team leader proceeds to lay out the problem, asking for it to be resolved. If private mediation is necessary, then that process can be used to resolve the conflict according to very strict guidelines. I happen to own a small stuffed moose for this very reason.

Communication Tip Summary #5:
Understand Competition & Practice Collaboration

- Women need to understand the competitive nature of business and at the same time gain the skills for collaboration and conflict resolution.
- Collaboration is the first step in resolving conflict situations.
- Put the Moose on the Table is one tool for resolving initial team-related conflicts.

Invite the Difficult Person To The Table

> The person who can most accurately describe reality without laying blame will emerge the leader."
>
> Susan Scott, *Fierce Conversations*. (New York: Berkley Books), 2004.

On almost every team, there is a person who is or becomes "difficult" to work with, to communicate with, or hard to persuade to do what you wish her to do. Using all your advanced communication skills, there will be a time when you must resolve a conflict with this person for the good of the team. Whenever any unresolved problem is left on the table, it grows exponentially! And, it becomes the proverbial "moose on the table", a very large, stinky mess. Thus, one of the major communication skill sets you will need is to handle these situations when they arise, before the moose becomes out of control.

Here is the perfect true example of how the President of the company let this get out of hand, losing a valued employee:

A new professional salesperson was hired at the X Factor Co. (small business looking to expand.) The President hired Joe with the sole purpose of expansion and growth, giving him a generous allowance and sales goal. He promised him that Joe could talk with him at any time and that Joe would get full cooperation from everyone in the company.

Joe was going along pretty well with an Operations person who handled his orders and made sure he was supported. With no warning, he was assigned a new person who, unknown to Joe, had been with the company 7 years and had wanted his job—from that point on, he sabotaged Joe at every turn. Finally, Joe was fed up with this and went to the President and told him of the situation. The President went to the new Operations Guy/Sabotager and told him what Joe had said about not getting support. Things did not change—in fact, worsened for several months, until Joe started looking around for a better job. He found one and promptly said goodbye to the President.

At the Exit Interview, Joe asked the President why he handled the situation the way he did, because he really did not want to leave. "Well, xxx has been with us all these years, and we know he's a pain in the butt, but if the truth be told, I don't like to confront him, and if I did, he'd make it that much harder on all of us."

(Special note: 4 salespeople have left the co. in the space of 2 years . . .)

This situation is a perfect example of how the "difficult" person knew he had the power to upset the group and intimidate anyone new who bucked his influence. If this has been handled correctly by the President, he would have used his advanced communications skill set to resolve this conflict AND keep the new salesperson.

The Skill Set To Invite The Difficult Person To The Table:

Listening For Information, Clarification, and Empathy

Building on Point 8, you need to be using this skill set until it is like breathing. You must be able to "switch" from one skill to the next, depending on what comes at you. Just as in a soccer match, the ball is going one way, and then suddenly there is a switch in tempo, and it travels back to the other goal. It is very important to be able to be nimble using these skills, knowing what you are doing as it happens.

When asking for feedback, prepare yourself for some surprises. Women have a tendency to ask for feedback from their friends with the idea of receiving support. In my opinion, this tendency does not prepare them for the "real" feedback you can receive at work. And, if this feedback contains criticism, many women are unprepared to receive it.

We need to ask for feedback, especially if we want to know how our performance is being viewed by our supervisor or team leader. Some companies have quarterly reviews—others do not. However, one thing is for sure—do not wait for an entire year to find out how your performance is being viewed. I believe that every 3-4 months you need to ask for feedback.

Questioning/Probing Skills

Women need to ask more probing questions; there is a tendency not to "hurt" someone's feelings and to be indirect. Be direct. Ask the tough questions that hang in the balance. Be courageous and probe until you get to the "real" problem. You are not naïve, and you need to get to the truth of the matter with anticipated questions before the session begins. Anticipate the answers. Anticipate your next move. Be strategic and bold when it comes to having this conversation.

Questions developed by Susan Scott and PJ Pierce:

- "I hear that the Operations Manager may be the reason you are leaving? I sense that it's part of the problem—what are the other parts, in your opinion?"
- "If you could stay with us, what situations and/or people would you change?"
- What topic are you hoping I won't bring up?
- What is currently impossible to do that, if it were possible, would change everything?
- What area under your responsibility are you most satisfied with? Least?
- What part of your responsibilities are you avoiding right now?

- What is your plan for your weakest employees?
- What conversations are you avoiding right now?
- If you were hired to consult with our company, what would you advise?

Understanding and Using Behavior, Consequences and Feelings Structure

Verderber and Verderber (2003) suggest that people, whatever, the situation, use the following advanced communication skill set pattern that includes Behavior, Consequences, and Feelings (BCF).

Discuss with the person about his or her *behavior* in specific, unemotional, non-blaming terms:

"Sean, you were very late tonight, after you promised to be in by midnight."

Discuss what the *consequences* were to you and others:

"As a result, your father and I waited up for you when it went past the midnight deadline—your sister was worried, because she knows that's not your usual pattern, and the dog was pacing for hours."

Discuss your *feelings* regarding this behavior:

"We felt violated, because you knew I had to get up early for an important business meeting presentation, and your father is flying out at 10:00 for a week. We felt that you did not care about the family's needs, only your own."

This conversation in many homes/offices is avoided, because of what the fallout may be; many times it is more important to keep the peace, and women may have learned this to be the way of conflict resolution in their own home. The issue gets swept under the rug and is never resolved until it's too big to confront.

Nip it in the bud. Confrontation is not always easy, but it is necessary to listen, to honestly communicate what the behavior is, the consequences to everyone around this person, and your feelings on the subject. I believe women need to assess their own conflict resolution patterns learned at home, because those translate into the workplace.

Susan Scott also provides several helpful steps in issue resolution:

- Name the issue.
- Select a specific example that illustrates the behavior or situation you want to change.
- Describe your emotions about this issue and clarify what is at stake.
- Identify your contribution to this problem and indicate your wish to resolve the issue.
- Invite your partner to respond and ask what have we learned and has anything been left unsaid.
- Make an agreement and decide how you will be responsible for keeping it.

Susan Scott, *Fierce Conversations*. (New York: Berkley Books), 2004.

I have used both processes at work and at home, and I feel that learning these processes has helped me grow as a manager. As a result, I hope that it will help with retention and happier work teams. The most important point is not to shy away from conflict—accept it as a part of the work day, and use your skill set to calm the waters with honest communication.

Another opportune time for a good discussion is the Performance Assessment.

Use the BCF structure which allows for an assessment that is clear, concise, and everyone knows what he or she needs to do to improve. I've used this technique in performance assessments and critiques for years with great success.

Take each work objective and:

- **Offer Strengths**
  *Specific **Behavior(s)** that are exceptional*
  ***Consequence** to the team's results*
  Feelings

- **Areas for Change w/timetable**
  ***Specific Behavior(s)** for change, based on professional growth*
  ***Consequence** to the team's results*
  Feelings

Note:

The Areas for Change may lead to the difficult conversation, and you must be ready for that to happen. Pull out your anticipated questions, prepare yourself for strong feedback, and hold your ground with facts. Women, prepare for that feedback and learn to listen for the "real" problem. Accept the feedback as that person's reality.

If that reality is upsetting another in your workgroup, and it has not been dealt with, mediation may be the only way to try to resolve the situation.

We must prepare for that eventuality. A simple mediation can be completed by you before you ask the professionals to step in. If the situation continues, then it is time for the Human Resources person to be involved and hire the mediator.

Mediation Process:

Mediation is one of the best ways of using your skills in the areas of listening, clarifying, probing, encouraging, praising, opinion giving, proposing a procedure or process, summarizing, paraphrasing, all the while acting as a neutral and impartial guide and helping structure an interaction that helps the conflicting parties find a mutually-acceptable solution to their problems. That's why there is so much respect for managers who can achieve this level of communication expertise. I have every positive expectation that you can do it!

Successful Mediation Techniques

1. Make sure the parties start with wanting to work the problem out.
2. Identify real conflict.
3. Maintain neutrality.
4. Keep discussion focused on issue(s) rather than personalities.
5. Give each equal "*air time*."
6. Keep discussion on solutions, not blame.
7. Have both parties support and fully understand the solution.
8. Give action plan & timeline.
9. Outline the follow-up procedure with specific behaviors to have responsibility for during the next conversation.

Verderber, Kathleen S. and Rudolph F. Verderber (2003).

Just for practice, imagine the following Situation, and go through the Mediation steps to resolve:

#1: Someone in your office is causing drama in the project planning sessions. This project is very important to the success of the office.

Person #1 is an inductive and wants every detail discussed. This person is taking too much time for Person #2 and the rest of the team. However, this person is also telling others outside the project room that Person #2 is "difficult to work with," which has Person #2 in a tizzy.

It has now reached crisis stage, and both have been called in separately to see the manager, which is ineffective. It's time to work through the situation together with your Mediation Process. Try this with a colleague, and see if you can resolve the situation! It works!

Communication Tip #6 Summary :
Invite The Difficult Person To The Table

❖ You must have courage and skill to confront and have the difficult conversation, which may be necessary to get to the next level of communication.

❖ The ability to clearly state the Behavior, Consequences, Feelings (BCF) to another person is a very important communication skill set for women to learn and use at work and at home—it can change your life.

❖ If you are skillful in managing conflict, you have advanced communication skills. It takes courage, skill, and a collaborative mindset.

❖ Put the Moose on the table and have the necessary conversation.

❖ Mediation is one of the most advanced communication skill sets you can master. Practice at work and at home for resolving conflicts. If they cannot be resolved by this method at work, please consult the HR Department to bring in a professional mediator.

Mind Your P's and Q's

Business Etiquette:

- Demonstrates "respect" for the other person, male or female
- Demonstrates your professionalism
- Shows your understanding and respect for different cultures
- Gives you a competitive edge overall
- Offers women the knowledge that manners count
- Provides that communication skills (presenting, phone, emails, writing, entertaining, facilitating meetings, working in cubes, interpersonal, etc.) as well as the essential business skills, are necessary to have workplace success

Paraphrased from materials of Ann Marie Sabath. *At-Ease,* Cincinnati, OH, 2002 and *Business Etiquette*, 1998.

Business Etiquette is an important area for women—many interviews are now held at lunch or dinner, and putting your best foot forward is always essential. Ann Marie Sabath, well-known consultant in the area of business etiquette, certified me in Chicago several years ago. As part of her programs, she routinely provides lunch as part of her presentations—nothing like on-the-job practice and expert information! Her materials are available—see Resources.

I created the following protocol quiz. Answers to the quiz are in the Summary.

So You Think You Know Your Protocol!!

1. *When you finish eating, American style, where should your knife and fork be to signal the server that you are finished?*

2. *If you are eating Continental style, where should the fork and knife be to signal the server that you are finished?*

3. *If you are finishing a bowl of rice in Japan, how are the chopsticks arranged to signal the server that you are finished?*

4. *At a lunch or dinner, what is the function of the fork that has been placed at the top of the plate?*

5. *How do you pass the cream and sugar or a pitcher of water to another?*

6. *What do you do with the pesky olive pit?*

7. *When a man is introduced to a woman in a business setting, who extends their hand first? What should you do in a semi-awkward moment when you realize the host has forgotten your name?*

8. *Should women apply lipstick at the lunch/dinner table? Yes _____ No _____*

9. *Scenario: introducing in a business setting. The man is your client, and the woman is your supervisor? Who do you introduce first?*

10. *Who gets out of the elevator and/or revolving door first, man or woman?*

11. *When speaking to a group of business women, is it appropriate to refer to them as* ladies?

12. *What gift do you NEVER give to your Chinese client? (Make sure that whatever you do give is wrapped very carefully—the wrapping is as important as the gift.)*

For you who would like to learn more about the area of business protocol, the following book was very helpful to me when I was traveling for a Fortune 100 company:

Do's and Taboos Around the World for Women in Business by Roger E. Axtell with assistance from: Tami Briggs, Margaret Corcoran and Mary Beth Lamb. See Resources for details.

Communication Tip #7 Summary : Mind Your P's & Q's

Business Etiquette:

- Demonstrates "respect" for the other person, male or female
- Demonstrates your professionalism
- Shows your understanding and respect for different cultures
- Gives you a competitive edge overall
- Offers women the knowledge that manners count
- Provides that communication skills (presenting, phone, emails, writing, entertaining, facilitating meetings, working in cubicles, interpersonal, etc.) as well as the essential business skills, are necessary to have workplace success

Answers to the Protocol Quiz:

1. Americans should signal the waiter that they are finished with the knife and fork diagonally on the plate at the 3 o'clock toward the 7 o'clock position.
2. The Continental style is the same as the American style of finishing.

3. The chopsticks should be placed across the center of the bowl, left to right, never pointing at the person sitting across from you.
4. That fork is for dessert.
5. You pass the cream/sugar and/or pitcher handle first so that the other person can grab it.
6. You place the olive pit in your napkin and deposit it discreetly on a plate or leave it in your napkin.
7. The man extends his hand, and if he doesn't, the woman immediately extends hers and mentions her name.
8. No application of lipstick at the lunch/dinner table.
9. You introduce your supervisor to the client. John (client), I'd like you to meet my supervisor Ann Hathaway. Ann, this is John Walton from xx Co."
10. The man goes out of the elevator first with the express objective of holding the doors open for the women—same in a revolving door—the man goes first to make it easier for the woman.
11. Ladies is fine with most women. Women should be used in the context of the presentation.
12. Never give a clock or wrist watch to a Chinese client—it is considered rude in the Chinese culture to remind anyone of the time that is lost.

Summary

What Your Counterparts Have Said

"Stick to the facts first when you are communicating—stories are secondary and could be used in training as examples but are not appropriate when asked a direct question."

Professional Women's Communication Skills Survey answer, 2009.

As I travel around the country, more and more women are sharing their expertise with other women, allowing a unified, professional brain trust to emerge. One of my colleagues has weekly Mastermind conference calls with her peers—they discuss everything from strategy to marketing tips to handling a difficult colleague. It has changed her life, knowing that there are other entrepreneurs out there who are struggling with the same situations.

In addition, she and I have designed a website that addresses women's personal and professional training needs. *www. ladieswholead.org* We talk with many outstanding women who are only too happy to help give contacts, mentoring advice, and marketing opportunities. Indeed, it is a competitive world, but at the same time women are "getting" the idea of networking instead of competing with each other. In a world where women were taught to compete for a man's attention and to compete in the social arena (clothes, friends, etc.), it is very refreshing to see how women are coming together to help one another.

In the latest government Job Statistics Report, women are now 47% of the workforce and growing. If that is the case, women should mentor and assist other women as they grow into positions of power. And, once they get that power, they need to have mentoring on how to use that power sparingly and carefully. Example: my son was speaking to one of the executives in the hallway, and a woman of power came down the hallway to speak to the executive as well. Because she had more power than my son, she tapped her foot, rolled her eyes, and kept up this bad behavior for quite a while. The male executive gave his time to my son, most likely to give her a small lesson in humility. Learn how to handle power once it's given and respect the people you are leading. Learn to handle teamwork without taking it all on your shoulders—learn to delegate, and learn to credit other people's work.

So, as a final summary, the following are the major points men conveyed to me, offering their thoughts honestly in a spirit of helpfulness. I wrote the book before I surveyed on purpose—so that my thoughts on the subject might stay separate, but hopefully be a confirmation of what I believe. I've been hearing about women's communication skills for years from male colleagues, and this book is now that confirmation.

Please evaluate their thoughts, and then it's your turn. I have placed a copy of the survey on page 72 that you can return to me that will be of help in my next book regarding communication tips for professional men! (Survey detail in Appendix C.)

What Your Male Counterparts Are Saying:

- Drama is not welcome in business dealings.
- Keep emotion to a minimum—too much right under the surface.
- I would like to see women not take every comment personally.
- Leadership is how much you can delegate—Let me *do it all* the "Right Way" is not my idea of delegation.
- Leadership and power is a privilege, not a way to emotionally abuse other subordinates, male or female.
- Control and respect the power you have.
- Sometimes I see Miss Perfect who cannot make mistakes and cannot acknowledge one.

- I would like to have women be flexible in a crisis and approach it in a way that communicates that all is under control.
- I would like to see assertive but not aggressive.
- I would like to see more confidence during a presentation instead of apologies.
- I would like to have more directness instead of beating around the bush.
- I would like to see women not press so hard but learn to understand the informal "rules of play"—all they need to do is ask.

Thank you for the opportunity to present these tips to you! I hope they have been helpful. If I can be of service to you in the future, please do not hesitate to contact me with your questions or comments.

Remember: Be brief in your explanations, "Net it out" when dealing with our male colleagues, and work diligently on not making it so personal, even though that is easier said than done!

PJ Pierce,Ph.D.

Ppierce3@woh.rr.com

Appendix A

Resources

American Management Association, *www.amanet.org*, 2009.

Axtell, Roger E. with Briggs, Tami; Corcoran, Margaret; and Lamb, Mary Beth. *Do's and Taboo's Around The World For Women in Business*. New York: John Wiley & Sons, 1997.

Braiker, Harriet B. *The Disease To Please*. Mc-Graw Hill, 2001.

Charan, Ram and Colvin, Geoffrey. Why CEO's Fail, *Fortune Magazine*, 2002.

Dumaine, Deborah. *Writing For Corporate Success*. (New York: Random House), 2001.

Dyer, Wayne. *Pull Your Own Strings* (New York: Morrow Press), 2002.

Gass, Robert H. and John S. Seiter. *Persuasion, Social Influence, and Compliance Gaining.* 2nd ed. (New York: Allyn and Bacon), 2003.

Griffin, Jack. *How To Say It At Work.* (New York: Prentiss Hall), 1998.

Harris, Thomas and Sherblom, John C. *Small Group and Team Communication.* (Allyn and Bacon, Boston, Massachusetts) 2002.

Hay, Louise. Empowering Women. (Carlsbad, California: Hay House Inc.), 1997.

Eisenhardt, Kathleen M., Jean L. Kahwajy, and L.J. Bourgeois III. "How Management Teams Can Have a Good Fight." *Harvard Business Review On Effective Communication*. (Boston, MA: Harvard Business School Press), 1997, reprint # 97402.

Perlman, Alan M. *Perfect Phrases for Executive Presentations*. (New York: McGraw-Hill), 2006.

Sabath, Ann Marie. *Business Etiquette in Brief*. (Cincinnati, Ohio, At Ease, Inc., 1995). For brochure purchase, contact atease@eos. net.

Schrank, Louise Welsh. *Gender and Communication: She Talks: He Talks*. (Lake Zurich, IL: The Learning Seed), 2004.

Scott, Susan, *Fierce Conversations*. (New York: Berkley Books), 2004.

Verderber, Kathleen S. and Rudolph F. Verderber. *Inter-Act: Interpersonal Communication Concepts, Skills, and Contexts*. 9th ed. (Belmont, CA: Wadsworth/Thompson Learning), 2003.

Professional Women's Communication Skills

If you had the opportunity to give advice to female professionals regarding their communication skills at work, what advice would you give them?

Writing (Reports, etc.)

Listening (Groups, meetings, etc.)

Presenting

Teaming

Conflict Resolution

Performance Assessments

Professional Communication

Other

Please return your observations/advice for your female counter parts to: PJ Pierce @ *ppierce3@woh.rr.com* for the next edition of *Women in Business*: *7 Successful Communication Tips To Enhance Your Career*.

Professional Men's Communication Skills

If you had the opportunity to give advice to male professionals regarding their communication skills at work, what observations/ advice would you give them?

Writing (Reports, etc.)

Listening (Groups, meetings, etc.)

Presenting

Teaming

Conflict Resolution

Performance Assessments

Other

Please return your observations/advice for your male counter parts to: PJ Pierce @ *ppierce3@woh.rr.com* for the next edition of *Men in Business*: 7 Communication Tips To Enhance Your Career.

Appendix D

Special Acknowledgements

Thank you for your support:

Mary Ann (MAK)
Clee
Paul
Arianne
Tara
Noah
Fred
Geoffrey
Aaron
Carrie
Edna
De Ann
Susan
Carolyn
Pat R. (Ruby)
Pat M. (Marquise)

Christine Martinello from Ladies Who Lead Group © *www. ladieswholead.org*

University of Dayton's Center for Leadership and Executive Development: Lisa, Becky, & Bob

Centerville Noon Optimist International Club

Cover Illustration by Jane

Xlibris Editors